MOTORCYCLE RACES

MOTORCYCLE MANIA

David and Patricia Armentrout

Rourke
Publishing LLC
Vero Beach, Florida 32964

www.rourkepublishing.com

PHOTO CREDITS: Cover ©Hugo Neto; title page and pp. 20 ©Daniel Gustavsson; pp. 4, 5, 19, 21 ©BMW; pp. 6 ©Putchenko Victorovich; pp. 7 ©Keith Robinson; pp. 8 ©Ovidiu Sopa; pp. 9, 17 ©Pascal Janssen; pp. 10 ©Dan Brandenburg; pp. 11 ©Phillip W Hubbard; pp. 12 ©Zdorov Vladimirovich; pp. 13 ©Drazen Vukelic; pp. 14 ©Steve Bruhn; pp. 7, 15, 19 ©Yamaha; pp. 16 ©Kawasaki; pp. 22 ©Honda Media.

Title page: *Racers are packed tightly together at the start of an enduro.*

Editor: Robert Stengard-Olliges

Cover design by Nicola Stratford

Library of Congress Cataloging-in-Publication Data

Armentrout, David, 1962-
 Motorcycle races / [David and Patricia Armentrout].
     p. cm. -- (Motorcycle mania II)
 ISBN-13: 978-1-60044-589-7
 1. Motorcycle racing--Juvenile literature. I. Armentrout, Patricia, 1960- II. Title.
 GV1060.A74 2008
 796.7'5--dc22
                          2007016378

Printed in the USA

CG/CG

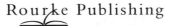

Rourke Publishing

www.rourkepublishing.com – rourke@rourkepublishing.com
Post Office Box 3328, Vero Beach, FL 32964

TABLE OF CONTENTS

RACING

Ready, set, GO! Three simple words that make us sit up and take notice. Why? Because they mean a race is about to begin.

People race just about anything that moves. Whether it's a creature or a machine, if it can go from point A to point B somebody will race it.

Motorcycles are no exception. The first motorcycle race likely began the first time two riders found themselves side by side.

A young racer works the course.

Riders line up at the starting line.

One of the great things about motorcycle racing is that almost anyone can do it. That's not to say it does not take skill. It takes hard work and commitment to be an **elite** racer. But motorcycle racing is fun, and not just for the pros. Kids and adults of all ages participate in motorcycle racing events all over the world.

The best motorcycle racers usually learn their sport at an early age.

Road races are very popular in Europe.

Racers lean into curves to maintain speed.

THE TRACKS

Where do people race motorcycles? Almost anywhere. Motorcycles are very versatile machines. Riders race them up steep hills, over rough off-road trails, around prepared tracks, and on public roads. Racing courses, or tracks, are built on dirt, mud, sand, snow, ice, and pavement.

A mud pit challenges the rider and his machine.

A crowd gathers to watch a motocross race.

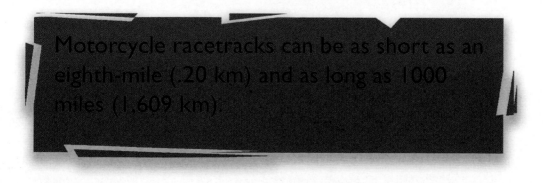

Motorcycle racetracks can be as short as an eighth-mile (.20 km) and as long as 1000 miles (1,609 km).

DRAG RACING

Motorcycle drag racing is a sport of pure speed—an **acceleration** contest. Two riders line up side-by-side and race on a straight track called a drag strip. Most drag races are a quarter-mile long.

Drag racers compete based on the class of motorcycle they ride. Pro Stock, Top Fuel, Super Sport, and Street E.T. are a few racing classes. The fastest dragsters reach speeds greater than 200 miles (321.87 km) an hour in less than seven seconds. Don't blink or you might miss the race!

Professional and amateur drag races are loud and exciting.

A wheelie bar at the rear of the bike keeps it from flipping during fast starts.

SPEEDWAY RACING

Speedway motorcycle racing is action packed and extreme. Unlike most motorcycles, speedway bikes have no gears and amazingly, no brakes! Riders race around short oval tracks made of loosely packed shale, dirt, grass, or ice. In a move called a power slide, riders slide their rear tire sideways around turns. The power slide helps them control speed without sacrificing power. Racers are able to quickly regain speed on the straight-aways.

A speedway racer power slides his way around a turn.

A sidecar team leans into a turn.

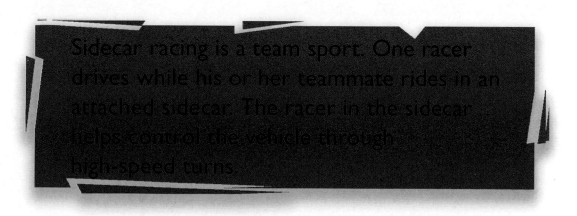

Sidecar racing is a team sport. One racer drives while his or her teammate rides in an attached sidecar. The racer in the sidecar helps control the vehicle through high-speed turns.

OFF-ROAD RACING

If you don't like to get dirty, then you should probably avoid **motocross**. Motocross is down and dirty, off-road racing. Tracks have numerous turns, bumps, jumps, mud pits, and other natural and man-made obstacles. **Spectators** are always in for a show as riders demonstrate their bike handling skills on challenging courses.

The checkered flag marks the finish line of a motocross race.

A motocross rider gets big air as he works his way around the course.

Supercross is a type of motocross race held on man-made, indoor courses. Popular in the United States, supercross is known for its steep jumps, **berms**, and next to impossible obstacles. Only experienced riders attempt to race on these extreme courses.

Supercross races are commonly held in large sports arenas or stadiums.

Supermoto racers use their inside foot for balance and control.

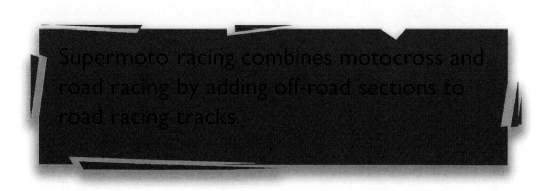

Supermoto racing combines motocross and road racing by adding off-road sections to road racing tracks.

ROAD RACING

Motorcycle road racing includes a number of different racing events. Road racing competitions are held on closed **circuit** racetracks or on closed public roads.

Sportbikes and superbikes are production road motorcycles. Both are high performance motorcycles capable of incredible speed. Their combination of speed and maneuverability is perfect for road racing. Sportbikes and superbikes are raced with or without **modifications**, depending on race rules.

The World Championship Grand Prix series is the highest motorcycle racing level. Grand Prix motorcycles are built only for racing and have little in common with production bikes.

Plastic or leather pads called sliders protect a rider's knees when cornering.

Grand Prix motorcycles are purpose-built machines used only for racing.

ENDURO

Enduro courses are mostly off-road, but may include portions on roadways. For this reason, enduro bikes must be street legal.

Some enduro courses cover just a few miles, but most are much longer. However, the object is not to see who finishes first; riders are judged on their ability to reach checkpoints on time. Enduros test a rider's endurance and riding skill.

Enduro racers plow through mud pits on their way to the next checkpoint.

Enduro bikes may be street legal, but they are built to handle just about any terrain.

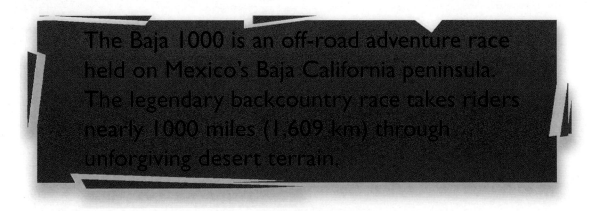

The Baja 1000 is an off-road adventure race held on Mexico's Baja California peninsula. The legendary backcountry race takes riders nearly 1000 miles (1,609 km) through unforgiving desert terrain.

WHAT'S YOUR PASSION?

Motorcycle racers have different reasons for loving their sport. Some love the thrill of blazing speed. Some enjoy the challenge of demanding terrain, and others crave the adventure of long distance racing. No matter the reason, motorcycling racers seem to have one thing in common; they love riding fast bikes.

Off road racing is physically demanding, but loads of fun!

GLOSSARY

acceleration (ak SEL uh ray shun) — increase in the rate of speed

berm (BERM) — a banked wall of earth

circuit (SUR kit) — a route that starts and finishes at the same place

elite (ih LEET) — a group of people considered the best in a particular category

modifications (MOD eh fuh KAY shunz) — changes made

motocross (MOE toe kross) — cross-country motorcycle racing

spectator (SPEK tay tor) — a person who watches

INDEX

FURTHER READING

Shuette, Sarah L. *Harley-Davidson Motorcycles*. Capstone Press, 2006.
Norman, Tony. *Motorcycle Racing*. Gareth Stevens Audio, 2006.
Schwartz, Tina P. *Dirt Bikes: Motocross Freestyle*. Capstone Press, 2004.

WEBSITES TO VISIT

http://www.worldsbk.com
http://www.amaproracing.com
http://www.motogp.com

ABOUT THE AUTHORS

David and Patricia Armentrout specialize in writing nonfiction books for young readers. They have had several books published for primary school reading. The Armentrouts live in Cincinnati, Ohio, with their two children.